YOGA
for Beauty
and Health

by Eugene S. Rawls
and Eve Diskin

**WARNER
PAPERBACK
LIBRARY**

A Warner Communications Company

WARNER PAPERBACK LIBRARY EDITION

First Printing: *August, 1968*
Second Printing: *May, 1969*
Third Printing: *December, 1970*
Fourth Printing: *June, 1972*
Fifth Printing: *February, 1974*

This Warner Paperback Library Edition is published
by arrangement with Prentice-Hall, Inc.

Cover photograph by Hugh Bell

Warner Paperback Library is a division of Warner Books, Inc.,
75 Rockefeller Plaza, New York, N.Y. 10019.

Ⓦ A Warner Communications Company